Have fun with this Book
Love Hannah
+ her mom :)

Holy
MYSTERIES!

Under the direction of Romain Lizé, CEO, Magnificat
Editor, Magnificat: Isabelle Galmiche
Editor, Ignatius: Vivian Dudro
Translator: Janet Chevrier
Proofreaders: Kathleen Hollenbeck, Samuel Wigutow
Layout Designers: Thérèse Jauze, Patrick Leleux PAO
Production: Thierry Dubus, Sabine Marioni

Original French edition: *Sacrés Mystères*
© Mame, Paris, 2020
© 2021 by Magnificat, New York — Ignatius Press, San Francisco
ISBN Magnificat 978-1-949239-56-0 — ISBN Ignatius Press 978-1-62164-480-4

Sophie de Mullenheim   Solenne & Thomas

Holy MYSTERIES!

12 Investigations into Extraordinary Cases

MAGNIFICAT • Ignatius

CONTENTS

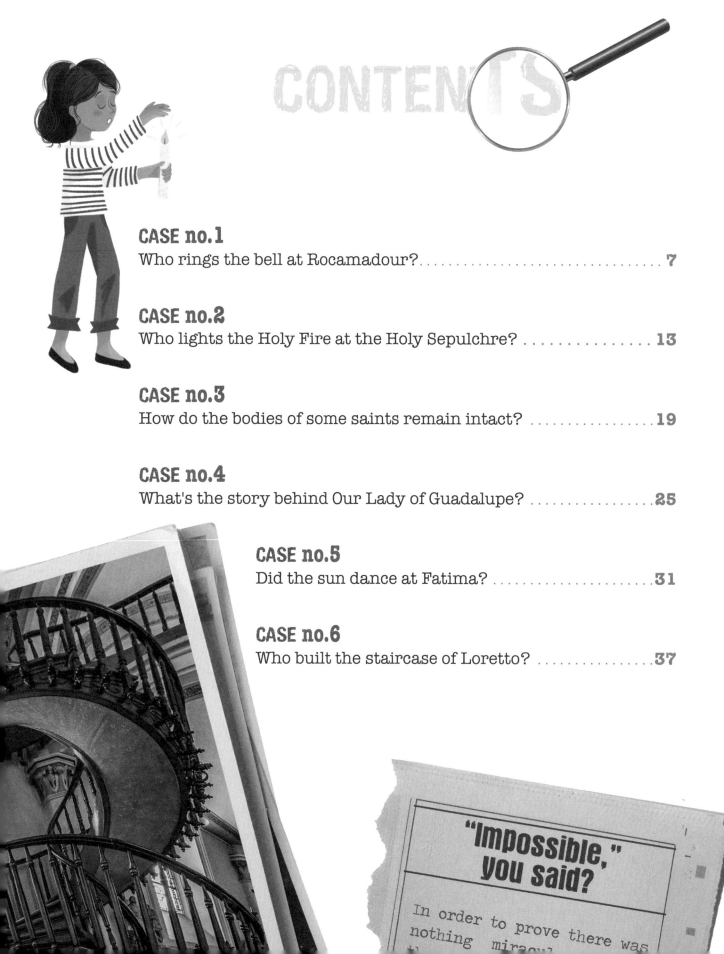

"Impossible," you said?

In order to prove there was
nothing miracu

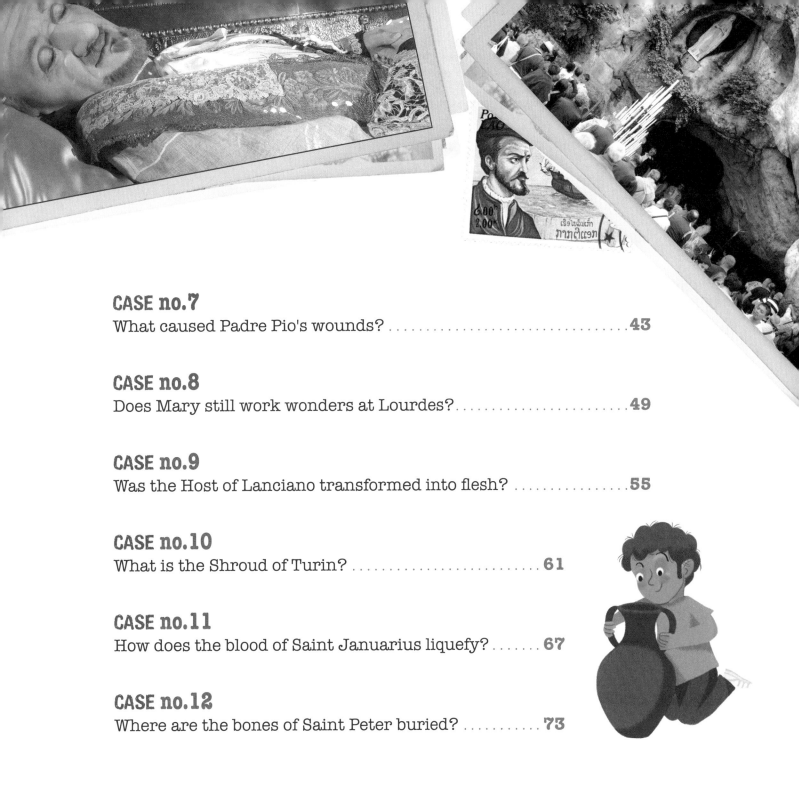

CASE no.1

Who rings the bell at Rocamadour?

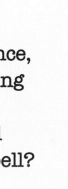

There isn't even a bell rope!

At Rocamadour, in the southwest of France,
a bell hangs from the high, vaulted ceiling
in the chapel of the Black Madonna.
Whenever it rings, a sailor is believed
to be rescued at sea. But who rings the bell?

The medieval village of Rocamadour sits on a rocky cliff about 400 feet above the valley below. For almost 900 years, pilgrims have flocked to this little town to venerate the Black Madonna, a dark wooden statue of the Virgin Mary holding Jesus on her lap. It's one of the oldest pilgrimage sites in France, and, strangely enough, many sailors visit it. Why? Because even though Rocamadour is more than 200 miles from the sea, the Black Madonna is thought to protect sailors.

Miniature Boats

In the little chapel with the Black Madonna, votive offerings line the walls. Engraved marble plaques bear the names of those who offer thanks to the Virgin of Rocamadour for answering their prayers. Some sailors

have hung models of their boats from the ceiling. Many were saved from shipwreck after they invoked the Black Madonna.

A Miraculous Bell

Right at the top of the chapel ceiling hangs a bell forged in iron. It is more than 1,100 years old and measures 9.5 inches long and 13 inches in diameter. Nothing links it to the ground, and there is no rope to ring it from below. And yet sometimes, mysteriously, the bell does ring. Each time, some believe, a miracle happens at sea. Sailors in danger are saved through the intercession of the Virgin of Rocamadour.

Perfectly Synchronized

In 2004, two women were praying in the chapel when they heard the bell ring. They immediately alerted a priest, who noted the day and the time in his notebook. A few months later, a man arrived with a model boat, to give thanks to the Black Madonna. On the day and at the exact time the priest had noted, the moment when the bell had rung, this man had prayed to Our Lady of Rocamadour and was saved from shipwreck.

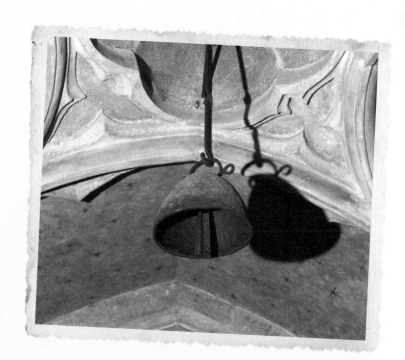

Holy
ANECDOTES!

What makes the bell ring?

A gust of wind? A bit of stone falling from the ceiling? Some invisible force? No one knows what makes the bell suddenly ring. The last time it rang was on September 29, 2008, but there was nothing supernatural about that. Due to work on the vaulted ceiling of the chapel, the priest had the bell removed and stored in the safety of his office. And he rung it there. At that same moment, two people on a boat ran into a violent storm off the coast of Morocco. The boat was doomed. In desperation, the two recited the prayer to Our Lady of Rocamadour, and they managed to survive! They went to Rocamadour to give thanks to the Virgin. But the story doesn't end there! Months later, during a guided visit, when the priest told the story of this event, another woman testified that on the same day, September 29, 2008, she too had been caught in the same storm off Morocco. She too had invoked heaven and had been saved!

 ## Why sailors?

Henry Plantagenet was very fond of the Virgin of Rocamadour, whose prayers, he believed, had cured him of a serious illness. He twice made a pilgrimage to Rocamadour. As he traveled through Brittany, this future King Henry II of England had an altar built in honor of Our Lady of Rocamadour near the Bay of Brest, an important seaport on the Atlantic coast. And so it was that she became the patron of sailors.

THE BLACK MADONNA

Our Lady of Rocamadour is nick-named the Black Madonna. Her statue indeed has a gray, blackish tint. But it wasn't always that way. This 12th-century Virgin was carved in walnut and originally covered in metal and precious gems. Alas, thieves and time gradually robbed it of its riches, leaving only the bare wood, which mysteriously darkened over the years.

 ## Once upon a time...

In 1535, the famous French navigator Jacques Cartier organized an expedition headed for Canada. He set off with three ships and 110 men. His plan was to sail up the Saint Lawrence River to penetrate the interior. But the expedition became stranded by the cold and the ice. Scurvy soon ravaged the crew: 25 men died of the illness, and most of the others were critically ill. Cartier prayed before an image of Our Lady of Rocamadour. He promised that, should she grant him the grace of survival, he would go on pilgrimage to venerate the Black Madonna. Soon after, Jacques Cartier met one of the local Indian chiefs, who told him how to make an herbal tea with the bark and leaves of a certain tree, now identified as the arborvitae. The cure worked, and the crew was saved. Cartier was true to his word and made the pilgrimage.

A STRANGE COLOR

Many scientists have tried to explain the dark color of the statue, but without success. All they can say is that it's not the result of the natural aging of the wood or of any kind of coating. Nor is the smoke from candles responsible for its color.

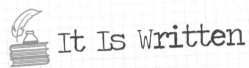

It Is Written

In the 12th century, to witness to the miracles performed by Our Lady of Rocamadour, a monk created the *Book of Miracles*. In this great register, all the miracles obtained through the intercession of the Black Madonna of Rocamadour are recorded. It lists 126. But this register was only kept for a few years, and it stops in 1172. To discover the supernatural interventions of the Virgin, we must look to the walls of the sanctuary. Large plaques indicate the main dates on which miracles are believed to have occurred.

Numerous Miracles

Some claim that the chapel bell rang for the last time in 1612. It announced the rescue of a Breton sailor named Jacques Jas and his crew, who had been caught in a violent storm. And yet, in 2004 and 2008, the bell rang again. The testimonies of rescues and healings are so numerous, and some so recent, that it would seem the Virgin of Rocamadour has worked wonders with or without the sign of the bell.

Prayer to Our Lady of Rocamadour

I stand before you, O Our Lady of Rocamadour,
who always hears the prayers
of those who have recourse to you.
Grant me bodily health
to serve God and those around me.
Grant also the same precious blessing
to those I love in this world.
I entrust to you all these lives that are dear to me.
Have pity on those who suffer
in their body or their soul,
O Mother of all.
With bodily health grant us spiritual wholeness.
In the midst of life's trials and worries,
keep our faith firm:
solid like the rock that shelters you
and where you welcome your children with such love.
Our Lady of Rocamadour, guard us, save us.
Amen.

11

CASE no.2

Who lights the Holy Fire at the Holy Sepulchre?

Without a lighter or matches!

Every year in Jerusalem, the same phenomenon occurs in the place where Jesus was laid in the tomb, the Holy Sepulchre. Before the Easter Vigil, on Holy Saturday, crowds gather to witness the wonder of the Holy Fire—an event that has taken place every year for more than a millennium.

The procedure is well established and takes place the same way every year to avoid anyone being accused of falsehood. It all begins on Good Friday, when the Israeli authorities search the little chapel built directly over the tomb of Jesus, inside the immense Basilica of the Holy Sepulchre. They make sure it contains nothing with which to light candles. They then surround the chapel in white tape sealed with fresh wax, which prevents anyone from entering undetected until noon the following day.

Alone in the Holy Sepulchre

On Holy Saturday, the Greek Orthodox patriarch of Jerusalem arrives in a procession accompanied by numerous priests and surrounded by a huge crowd. As the wax seals are removed, the patriarch is frisked by soldiers to make sure that he has nothing with him to light candles.

He then removes his priestly outer vestments and enters the chapel of the Holy Sepulchre, alone, with two tightly bound bunches of 33 thin, unlit candles. It is dark inside.

Holy Light

The patriarch begins to recite a long prayer. All around the chapel, the packed basilica hums with the prayer of the faithful. You can feel the tension as they wait until a blueish light rises from the tomb of Christ. The door of the chapel opens, and the patriarch emerges with his candles burning. Bells ring as cheers and cries of joy rise from the crowd.

The Fire Spreads

The patriarch then distributes the Holy Fire to the people who have been waiting, many of whom carry torches formed by 33 candles bundled together. The fire spreads from person to person until everyone's candles are lit. In some cases, people's candles light spontaneously. Some pilgrims are in a great hurry because they have planes to catch—to transport the Holy Fire to Orthodox churches around the world for their celebrations of the Easter Vigil!

Holy ANECDOTES!

 ## Why 33?

According to Christian tradition, this was Christ's age when he died on the cross, before rising again.

THE END OF TIME?

Some believe that the day the Holy Fire no longer descends, the end of the world is nigh. And yet there have been Easters when the miracle did not occur—perhaps because, at the time, the churches were in conflict with one another or controlled by hostile rulers.

 ## Once upon a time...

The miracle of the Holy Fire inside the Holy Sepulchre is not new. It's one of the oldest extraordinary events in Christianity to be the subject of testimonies. The first texts that speak of it date back to the 4th century. Today, it is broadcast live on television in all Orthodox countries.

☀ An unpredictable fire ☀

In 1579, the Turkish authorities who ruled the Holy Land would not allow the Greek patriarch to enter the church for the ceremony. According to Orthodox chroniclers, the patriarch stood near the entrance of the basilica, praying. Without warning, a marble column split open and out leapt the Holy Fire, from which the patriarch lit his candles. Today, one can still see the riven and charred column where this miracle is said to have taken place.

MIRACULOUS OR NOT?

Over the course of the centuries, many have questioned the miraculous nature of the Holy Fire. Skeptics say it's just a moneymaking fraud of the Orthodox Church. According to some, the patriarch takes advantage of the darkness to open a niche that hides a lighted lamp. For others, it's the clever result of chemicals that spontaneously ignite. These critics have to be taken seriously. However, those who try to explain it precisely struggle to agree on the method being used.

PROOF ON TV

In 2005, a Greek historian performed a demonstration on television using candles previously soaked in phosphorus. Without his doing anything more, after 15 minutes, the candles lit up by themselves! According to the historian, this explained the Holy Fire, especially as the properties of phosphorus have been known since before the Death and Resurrection of Jesus Christ. But then what explains the flashes of blue and white light that some people have claimed to have seen?

AN ELECTRIC ATMOSPHERE

In 2008, a Russian scientist decided to investigate the electric discharges that seemed to occur at the moment of the miracle. During the ceremony, for more than six hours, he measured the atmospheric electricity minute by minute. After analysis, he concluded that there was an electrical discharge at the moment of the descent of the Holy Fire. But he could not determine where this electricity comes from.

16

Live from the Holy Sepulchre

The Holy Fire can be traced through the centuries in many travel reports from the Holy Land. A Russian priest named Daniel described the "miracle of the sacred fire" and the ceremonies surrounding it in great detail in his travelogue from 1106-1107. He recalled how the patriarch entered the chapel with two unlit candles. He knelt in front of the stone on which Christ was laid after his death and said certain prayers, whereupon light emerged from the inside of the stone—a blue, indefinable light that after some time ignited the oil lamps and the patriarch's two candles.

 ## A Fire That Doesn't Burn

Pilgrims who light their candles from the Holy Fire often pass the flame over their hands and faces—a bit like they are washing themselves with the light. They also make sweeping signs of the cross with their candles. Some say the fire causes no burns—not on the skin, the clothing, or the hair. And this wonder lasts for 33 minutes! But any longer than that, and the fire burns sharply.

CASE no.3

How do the bodies of some saints remain intact?

Even when their coffins decompose...

When a person is about to be declared a saint, it's not uncommon for his or her body to be moved and reburied in a place where the person can more easily be venerated. Sometimes, when the tomb is opened, the body is found beautifully preserved.

In 680, all the members of Ely Abbey in England gathered for the great event about to take place. The mother abbess, the future Saint Sexburga, wished to have the bones of her sister Etheldreda moved from the abbey cemetery to the church. Etheldreda, who had died from the plague 17 years earlier, was the foundress of the abbey, and the monks and nuns felt that her remains deserved to be buried inside the church she had founded.

Numerous Witnesses

Everything was ready for the transferal. A large tent had been erected, and the monks and nuns were gathered in the courtyard, with the men on one side and the women on the other. Cynefrid, a physician, was present. Shortly before the death of Etheldreda, he had operated on her to remove a tumor from her neck. She had been left with a large scar that was still scarlet upon her death.

Amazement!

The tomb was opened, and the mother abbess approached with a few other nuns. It was she who was to clean the bones and place them in a casket to be taken into the church.

But when the coffin was opened, Sister Sexburga cried out in astonishment. A witness approached, along with other nuns. The body was intact! Etheldreda looked like she had only just fallen asleep. The doctor approached to see this wonder. He was amazed to observe that even the clothing of this holy woman was in a perfect state of preservation. But that wasn't what most surprised this man of science: on observing the body more closely, Cynefrid observed that the scar on her neck had disappeared. There remained not the slightest trace, as though it had never existed!

A Precious Memorial

This phenomenon excited the little community with great joy. The intact body was finally transferred to a tomb inside the church, and, little by little, pilgrims flocked to it. The foundress rapidly became one of the most popular saints in the whole country. The story of the discovery of Etheldreda's body was recounted by Bede the Venerable. His was one of the first accounts to memorialize the discovery of an incorrupt body. Since then, there have been many others.

Holy ANECDOTES!

IN NORMAL CIRCUMSTANCES...

It's estimated that a body buried in a coffin takes between eight and 10 years to decompose completely. Immediately after death, in about the first 10 hours, the body becomes rigid and cools down to ambient temperature. Three days later, it begins to decompose.

HE'S BLEEDING!

When Saint Francis Xavier died, his body was enclosed in a wooden box filled with quicklime to make the flesh decompose quickly, leaving only the bones. This was done in order to send his bones to Goa, India, where the saint had begun his mission of evangelization on the Indian subcontinent. Two months later, the quicklime was removed. But instead of the expected bones, the body of the saint was found perfectly intact. And when someone tried to remove a small piece of skin from his knee, blood flowed! Sixty years later, when one of the arms was removed from the corpse to be kept as a relic, the body bled again!

✳ A healthy complexion ✳

Saint Teresa of Àvila was buried in 1582 in a deep grave, and her body was covered with stones and lime. A few months later, since numerous miracles had occurred at her tomb and a violet perfume rose from the ground, it was decided to reopen the tomb and inspect her body. Her clothing had completely rotted away, but, once washed, the saint herself had the freshness of a person who had simply fallen asleep. Her skin was supple, elastic, and white.

> By the sweat of your face you shall eat bread, until you return to the ground, from which you were taken; For you are dust, and to dust you shall return.
>
> (Genesis 3:19)

Is it the soil?

Some claim that cases of incorruptibility are due to the composition of certain soils with unusual preservative properties. But how, then, to explain that sometimes the coffin has totally decomposed while the body itself remains intact—as in the case of Saint Catherine Labouré? And why does one body remain perfectly preserved while those around it have returned to dust?

What does the Church say?

As always when confronted by unexplained phenomena, the Church is very cautious. Just because a body is found in an excellent state of preservation doesn't necessarily mean the person is a saint.

CONTINUOUS OOZING

The body of Saint Charbel, a Lebanese saint who died in 1898, has never stopped oozing blood mixed with water. It has oozed so much that the clothing of his corpse has had to be changed several times! Even more astonishing, the liquid began seeping out of the tomb through fissures in the stone. No doctor who has observed the phenomenon firsthand has been able to explain it, especially since the amount of blood loss from the body since death far exceeds that normally contained in a healthy body.

All saints?

Do you have to be a saint to have an incorruptible body? It would seem not, since other bodies have been found in excellent condition after years spent buried in the ground. One famous example is King Henry IV of France, whose body was exhumed in 1793 during the French Revolution, 183 years after his death. His body was found to be dried out, but very well preserved and without a trace of decay. Unfortunately, his body was desecrated and thrown into a mass grave.

THE LIST IS LONG!

Saints Catherine Labouré, Padre Pio, John-Mary Vianney, Teresa of Ávila, Vincent de Paul, Josephine Bakhita... The list of saints whose incorrupt bodies can be venerated is long. Incorruptibles have been recorded throughout the centuries and across continents. Men and women, children and adults: each has a different story but the same serenity in death.

☀ Forever fresh? ☀

Incorruptibility isn't eternal! In fact, some bodies are found intact years after death, only to decompose after being repeatedly exhumed. Sometimes, incorruptibility can last a decade, and sometimes several centuries. The body of Saint Roseline de Villeneuve, who died in 1329, is reported to have remained intact for 565 years. In 1894, the body was attacked by insects and had to be embalmed.

23

IT ALMOST LOOKS LIKE WAX...

When people see a body preserved inside a glass case, they're often struck by the waxy look of the face and the hands. Is the saint really intact? Is that the real body? What if it's just a wax figure? Actually, the body is the real incorrupt body, but the face is covered with a layer of wax or silicon. This ensures that it remains in good condition when exposed to light, which makes it more fragile.

CASE no.4

What's the story behind Our Lady of Guadalupe?

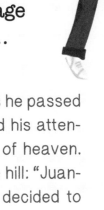

You would almost think the image of Mary is alive!

In Mexico, the enormous Basilica of Our Lady of Guadalupe houses an amazing treasure: a portrait of the Virgin Mary mysteriously imprinted on the fabric of a cloak. This image is far from having yielded all its secrets...

On December 9, 1531, Juan Diego was on his way to Mass. As he passed by the foot of the Tepeyac Hill, wonderful birdsong attracted his attention. He stopped, convinced that this music was a foretaste of heaven. It was then he heard a voice calling to him from the top of the hill: "Juanito!" This affectionate nickname touched Juan Diego, who decided to find out who was calling.

Such a Beautiful Lady!

When Juan Diego reached the top of the hill, he saw a young woman haloed with light. She introduced herself as the Virgin Mary, Mother of the True God, and she said it was to Juanito, the most humble of God's children, that she had chosen to reveal herself. She asked Juanito to go to the bishop and tell him to build a church on that very spot. The Virgin Mary promised to grant many graces to those who would come there to pray.

An Eager Messenger

Juan Diego immediately set off to carry out his mission. But the bishop was stubbornly skeptical. What kind of outlandish story was this? He didn't believe Juan Diego. So Juan Diego went straight back to the Virgin Mary to beg her to find a more important messenger to whom the bishop would listen. But the Blessed Virgin insisted: it was Juan Diego who must ask the bishop to build a church. Juan Diego obediently returned to the bishop, who listened to him again but still had doubts and demanded proof!

Flowers in Winter

Juan Diego explained the bishop's demand to the Virgin Mary. She told him to go gather roses from the top of the hill. But it was winter: December 12! Any flowers were rare there during that time of year, never mind roses. Yet, on the hilltop, Juan Diego found countless, beautifully scented roses. He gathered them up in his cloak—his tilma—and carried them to the Virgin Mary. Mary told him to show them to the bishop. These flowers would be the proof he was looking for!

A Miraculous Image

Juan Diego arrived at the bishop's palace, his cloak full of roses perfuming everything in his path. He had to wait a long time before the bishop received him. But he waited, and when he at last stood before the bishop, Juan Diego repeated the Blessed Virgin's instructions. Then he opened his tilma. The miraculous roses cascaded to the floor, revealing on his cloak an image of the Virgin Mary. Centuries later, the image is still admired and venerated in Mexico under the name of Our Lady of Guadalupe.

Holy
ANECDOTES!

A fictional character?

Some historians claim that Juan Diego never existed! Indeed, they believe the first real mention of him dates to more than a century after the apparitions. That's too late to be believed. But the account has also been found in the text of the writer Antonio Valeriano, which predates the death of Juan Diego.

I.D. CARD

Juan Diego was a native of the Chichimeca tribe. He was poor and deeply devout. He was baptized at the age of 50, seven years before the apparitions. Following these events, Juan Diego led the life of a hermit, living near the first chapel dedicated to the Virgin of Guadalupe. On July 31, 2002, he was canonized by Pope John Paul II. He is the first indigenous saint of the American continent. Juan Diego is celebrated on December 9, three days before the feast day of Our Lady of Guadalupe.

AN ARMY OF SCIENTISTS

Many scientists have studied the image of Our Lady of Guadalupe. Chemists, painters, surgeons, astronomers, ophthalmologists, doctors—all have made surprising discoveries that remain unexplained from the human point of view. And these aren't just any scientists. Some are members of the very serious and celebrated American space agency, NASA, no less!

What beautiful eyes you have!

The eyes of Our Lady of Guadalupe are one of the most astonishing mysteries about this image. Ophthalmologists have studied them and found in them the same properties as "living" human eyes. They're sensitive to light, and the images imprinted on their retinas are like those found in human eyes. Like the Church, scientists remain cautious. They observe the phenomenon but do not rule on whether it's supernatural. Nevertheless, the study of many eyes in other paintings or photographs is enlightening: the same phenomenon is found nowhere else.

Impossible, you said?

In order to prove there was nothing miraculous about the image, one man had an exact copy of the image made on coarse fabric and had it hung in the chapel next to the site of the apparitions. Seven years later, in 1796, the image was so degraded and faded that it had to be taken down.

SO HUMAN!

It's amazing that the fabric of the tilma has always remained at a temperature between 97.8 and 98.6°F. That's human body temperature! It remains yet another unexplained phenomenon.

PHOTOGRAPHY OF THE SKY

Astronomers can't explain it. In 1983, a study of the stars imprinted on the Virgin's mantle revealed that they are positioned exactly as they would have been in the sky over Mexico on the night of December 12, 1531.

A STRANGE PALETTE

One German, in 1936, and then two Americans, in 1979, studied the fibers of the tilma. They were amazed to discover that the fabric, although colored, contains no dye: neither animal, vegetable, nor mineral. In other words, its colors do not exist!

A REVOLUTIONARY FABRIC

The fabric of the tilma must be the envy of textile engineers. It's made of just a coarse cactus fiber (maguey), but despite its great age—nearly 500 years—it's still in excellent condition. More than that, it has not been damaged by insects or even by a workman who once spilled acid on it. It's even resisted bombs! In 1921, a man placed an explosive right underneath the image. The metal crucifix in front of the image was bent in two. But the image, its frame, and the fabric remained intact.

Breaking News
Hot off the Press

In 2014, one of the greatest specialists on the tilma of Guadalupe announced that there are thirteen figures imprinted in the eyes of the Virgin: an indigenous man, an old man (believed to be the bishop of Mexico), a young black man and woman, a bearded man, and Juan Diego. What's more, in the middle of the pupil, a group of seven other people appear who, in a separate scene, form a kind of family.

AN EXPECTANT MOTHER

The Virgin of Guadalupe is pregnant, which is indicated by the black sash, two ends of which are falling over her stomach. And other signs have been documented over the centuries. One day, a doctor placed a stethoscope on Mary's belly. He could hear a heart beating at 115 beats per minute, the same as the heartbeat of a baby in its mother's womb. Ophthalmologists have also discovered small, swollen veins at the back of the Virgin's eye, just like those observed in the eyes of pregnant women.

29

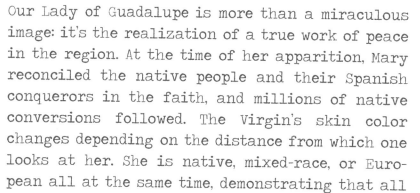

A Miracle of Peace

Our Lady of Guadalupe is more than a miraculous image: it's the realization of a true work of peace in the region. At the time of her apparition, Mary reconciled the native people and their Spanish conquerors in the faith, and millions of native conversions followed. The Virgin's skin color changes depending on the distance from which one looks at her. She is native, mixed-race, or European all at the same time, demonstrating that all men are equal in the eyes and the heart of God.

O MILAGRE DE FÁTIMA

Varios aspectos

...nomento de descobrir o sol e de se
...sionou a multidão.

...juntou a 13 de outubro. O teu
...ueres estabelecer uma opinião
...os como o meu, pois que es-
...em dificil, tal a de relatar im-
...os factos que diante de mim
...elucidativo a eles se pren-
...r satisfazer o teu desejo,
...nossos olhos e os nossos ou-
...ouviram coisas diversas, e
...ue ficaram insensiveis á
...espectaculo, unico en-
...onto digno de meditação

O que ouvi e
me levou a Fáti-
ma? Que a Vir-
gem Maria, de-
pois da festa da
Ascenção, apare-
cera a tres crian-
ças que apascen-
tavam gado, duas
...ocinhas e um
...galete, reco-
...endando-lhes
...orassem e
...entendo-lhes
...cer ali, so-
...ma azinhei-
...dia 13 de
...ez, até que
...ubro lhes
...alquer si-
...oder de
...aria re-
...Espa-
...nova
...leguas

CASE no.5

Did the sun dance at Fatima?

70,000 people are said to have seen it!

On October 13, 1917, a crowd gathered in a field near Fatima, Portugal. Three children had announced a miracle would occur, and many people had traveled to witness it. They were not disappointed, for the sun appeared to dance in the sky. It was amazing!

On May 13, 1917, during the First World War, three simple shepherd children reported seeing a lovely lady in a field near Fatima, Portugal. They said she asked them to pray the Rosary every day for peace and to return to that spot on the 13th of every month. News spread very quickly that the Virgin Mary was appearing to the children. There was great excitement, and, on July 13, at the third apparition, a large crowd gathered around the children. Some people still doubted the apparitions were real. So Lucia, the eldest of the children, asked Mary for a miracle. The Virgin promised that one would take place on October 13, 1917.

True to Her Word

On October 13, 1917, there was a dense crowd at the place of the appa-ritions. Seventy thousand had made the trip to be there! Among them were the three shepherd children, but also experts such as doctors, journalists, and photographers. Everyone wanted to see what would happen! And nothing could stop the believers, not even the rain that had been falling all morning. Suddenly, at midday, the sky changed. At 1:45 p.m., the rain stopped, the sun emerged from the clouds, and the miracle began!

A Strange Light

This was no ordinary sun. It looked like a flat, silvery, bright disc surrounded by a crown of sparkling rays. Strangely, one could look at the sun directly without discomfort, without it burning the eyes. And its light became colored in bright hues. The people, the plants, and the countryside took on all the colors of the rainbow.

The Dance of the Sun

Then, the sun began to move and spin rapidly. At one point, it seemed to detach itself from the sky and come dangerously close to the earth. *Was it about to hit?* Some screamed; some panicked. After about ten minutes, the sun returned to its usual place in the sky. It became still again, and its light was as blinding as ever. The sun had returned to normal.

Holy ANECDOTES!

A Key Witness

On the morning of October 13, 1917, the journalist Avelino de Almeida published an article making fun of the apparitions of Fatima. He cried foul and accused the people of being superstitious. Avelino de Almeida was anti-religious, and his newspaper was too. So, to prove the deception of the apparitions of Fatima, the journalist went there to await the supposed miracle.

Yet there was indeed an extraordinary event, and Avelino de Almeida wrote with honesty about what happened. He described the sun and its dance, the crowd that was present and its dispersal. A real eyewitness account, Almeida's article was published a few days later. It delighted Catholics but seriously annoyed the journalist's friends and provoked their very sharp criticism.

A WARNING FOR YOUR EYES!

When one stares too long at the sun, the retina is damaged and reacts by "imprinting" images that overlap and can give the impression that the sun is dancing. That's an attractive scientific theory, but it has its downside: a retina damaged by staring at the sun takes months to repair itself and sometimes never recovers. So what can explain why the thousands who witnessed this wonder suffered no eye problems afterward?

AN ECLIPSE?

The first theory that arose to explain the phenomenon was that it was a solar eclipse. But witnesses who had already experienced an eclipse said that this experience was quite different. And eminent scientists working in the observatory a few miles from the site had forecast nothing of the kind, let alone seen anything like it. For them, it was impossible that this was an astronomical phenomenon. An explanation had to be sought elsewhere.

CLOUD OR NOT?

The most probable and least far-fetched theory lies in the meteorological arena. Scientists state that the coincidence of several phenomena could explain the dancing sun. Such an occurrence requires a lens-shaped mass of air, countervailing winds to make the sun spin, and many ice crystals trapped in the air to reflect the light. Under these conditions, the sun could appear to be dancing in the sky. This explanation seems plausible, but no meteorologist has been able to say whether any such conditions were present on October 13, 1917.

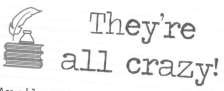

They're all crazy!

Another hypothesis has also been proposed: a collective hallucination. Told to expect a miracle, the witnesses were prepared to believe one was taking place. But then what? How do you explain that those who disbelieved in miracles saw the same things as everyone else?

HERE WE GO AGAIN...

Between October 30 and November 8, 1950, Pope Pius XII also saw the sun dance. He testified that on four different occasions he watched the sun spin in the sky without any blinding light. The timing of this wonder doesn't seem a question of chance: it occurred during the week he declared the dogma of the Assumption, affirming the ancient belief that God took Mary to heaven.

So what then?

Finally, according to Pio Scatizzi, a professor of astronomy, there remain only two possibilities since the nearby observatory had observed nothing abnormal on that day. Either the thousands of witnesses were duped at the same time and all gave false testimony; or, it was a supernatural phenomenon. Whatever the case, the Church remains highly cautious about such events. Although the Church has ruled that the apparitions at Fatima are worthy of belief, she is careful to leave everyone free to believe them, and the Miracle of the Sun, or not.

CASE no.6

Who built the staircase of Loretto?

So perfect it's like a miracle!

In Santa Fe, New Mexico, pilgrims flock to the Loretto Chapel. They don't come because it is the site of an apparition or the shrine of a saint. No, the faithful flock there to see... a spiral staircase.

At the end of the 19th century, the Sisters of Loretto, who had come to the region to open a school for girls, were having a chapel built. But in 1878, as work was just finishing, the Sisters of Loretto realized there was no staircase up to the choir loft!

A Call for Help

When the Sisters of Loretto realized the architect's mistake, they called upon local carpenters to build a staircase. But they all refused, explaining that there just wasn't enough room to build one. The space was too narrow. The only solution was to reach the choir loft with a simple ladder, which was not very convenient and was dangerous as well. The other option was to knock down the chapel and rebuild it again correctly.

Prayer Saves the Construction Site!

Far from becoming discouraged, the Sisters prayed to Saint Joseph for nine days. After all, wasn't he the patron saint of carpenters? On the last day of their novena, an old man turned up and offered to build the staircase. A few months later, the man disappeared without even being paid, leaving behind a magnificent spiral staircase of nearly impossible dimensions, a marvel to master carpenters even to this day. For the Sisters, there was no doubt that Saint Joseph himself had built it.

A Strange Kind of Workman

The Sisters of Loretto left several accounts concerning the project. They say that the staircase was built too quickly for one man alone with only simple tools, yet the Sisters never saw the man at work. Whenever they entered the chapel, he was either not there or resting. Was he perhaps an insomniac and preferred to work at night? As to whether the man was up to this colossal work all on his own, the Sisters reported that he never showed any signs of fatigue. Surprising, isn't it?

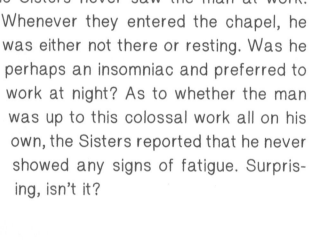

Holy ANECDOTES!

I.D. CARD

Who was the man who came to the aid of the Sisters of Loretto? No one knows; his identity remains a mystery. All that's known are a few details: he was old, had a white beard, and traveled on a donkey with a simple toolbox. That's not much to go on to carry out an investigation. All the more so as the man left without even asking for or receiving his pay. He simply disappeared without a trace.

At last, a lead!

In the 1990s, one writer announced that she researched and found a lead for the mysterious carpenter. He was thought to be a certain François-Jean Rochas, a Frenchman and expert woodworker. He lived at the time in the region of Santa Fe, and, according to his obituary, was the creator of the staircase of Loretto. Everything seemed to fit. Except that, in 1878, François-Jean Rochas had been twenty-seven years old, nothing like the old man with a white beard as described by the Sisters of Loretto.

IN NUMBERS

- Height of the staircase: 20 feet
- Number of complete twists: 2
- Diameter of the steps: 7 feet
- Height of the steps: 7 inches
- Number of steps: 33

Some of these numbers are astonishing, even symbolic. The number seven, to start with, figures very often in the Bible and is a sign of perfection. But above all, the number of steps, 33, matches the number of years Christ lived on earth.

AN IMPOSSIBLE CONSTRUCTION

Numerous architects have studied this beautiful construction to discover its secrets and each time are astonished by many of its elements. How could one man working alone with the rudimentary tools of the 19th century have achieved such a remarkable staircase? The curve of each step is absolutely perfect, as perfect as if it had been constructed using high-tech tools and machines.

✳ What is holding it up? ✳

40

Building a spiral staircase in New Mexico in the 19th century was unheard of. This type of staircase didn't exist in the region, and the method of construction hadn't been mastered by the local workmen. But the most astonishing thing about this staircase is that it has no central pole; that it stands upright is a wonder! Its entire weight is carried between the bottom and the upper step, attached to the choir loft above. Today, such a feat can probably be explained by the very tight twist of the staircase. In this way, the inner wooden spiral that the staircase forms as it winds around itself more or less serves as a central pole.

✳ No nails! ✳

Some proclaim a miracle because the staircase was built without nails or glue. The carpenter used only wooden joints. Nails were very expensive at the time, and wooden joints were used in many buildings in the region. However, as far as glue is concerned, it would seem it was replaced by some other material to hold the different pieces of the steps together. But what is that material? No one can say exactly.

What's that wood?

When the staircase of Loretto was finished and the carpenter had disappeared without a word, the Sisters worried about whom they were to pay for the wood used to build it. They asked around the sawmills in the area: Had the wood come from their warehouse? The answer was always the same: the wood hadn't come from them. No one knew where it came from!

Today, the origin of the wood remains a mystery. Some say it's acacia, while others, more numerous, lean toward spruce. Whatever the case, neither of these species of tree existed in that part of the United States at the time the staircase was built. Did the carpenter have it shipped from Europe?

In 1994, a study reopened the mystery. It confirmed that the wood in question is a species of cedar that grows in the Mediterranean, in the region of Israel and Palestine—in short, in the land of Jesus!

41

DOES IT EVER WEAR OUT?

At over 140 years old, the staircase doesn't seem to have changed since the day it was built. The wood looks astonishingly brand new. Indeed, over the course of the years, the steps should be at least a little worn, the same as stone stairs, for example. But they show nothing of the sort, despite the passage of so many footsteps. Just one more mystery to add to the rest!

CASE no.7

What caused Padre Pio's wounds?

They look like the wounds of Jesus on the cross...

The crucified then risen Jesus appeared to his Apostles after Easter. In his hands and feet, he bore the marks of the nails, and in his side the wound of the lance. These were the visible signs of his Passion. In the history of the Church, some saints have also been marked by these signs, called stigmata. Among them is Saint Pio.

The date was September 20, 1918. Padre Pio, a Capuchin monk in Italy, had just celebrated Mass. As he lingered, giving thanks at the foot of the altar, he was seized by a great tremor, followed by an indescribable kind of peace. The Lord then appeared to him, just as he had done a few days earlier. But this time, the Lord's hands and side were bleeding. Jesus was grieving the ingratitude of men lacking in love for him.

To Suffer with Christ

Padre Pio was overwhelmed by this vision of Jesus. He later recounted: "This revealed his suffering and his desire to unite souls with his Pas-

sion. He invited me to partake of his sorrows and to meditate upon them." Padre Pio understood the suffering and sorrow of Jesus. He asked Christ if he could do anything to ease his pain. The Lord told him, "I unite you with my Passion," and then disappeared. When Padre Pio emerged from his ecstasy, he found blood flowing from wounds on his hands, his feet, and his side.

With Total Discretion

On the day of the appearance of the stigmata, Padre Pio was still a very young priest: he was only thirty-one. The wound in his side bled continuously, but even more so from Thursday evenings to Saturday, in remembrance of the Passion. He avoided talking about this grace offered him by the Lord to share in his sufferings. He even tried to hide his wounds by wearing mittens to cover his hands. But it was all in vain. News spread like wildfire, and larger and larger crowds came to him to attend Mass and to confess their sins.

Right to the Very End

The stigmata of this holy priest lasted for exactly 50 years. For 50 years, he had tirelessly devoted himself to religious life, sacrifice, and love for the Lord. On September 22, 1968, Padre Pio celebrated a Mass on the occasion of the 50th anniversary of his stigmata. At 2:30 the following morning, after receiving the Sacrament of Anointing of the Sick, Padre Pio breathed his last. He was 81 years old and had just been united with the Lord he had loved so very much. A few hours after his death, the marks of the stigmata on his body mysteriously disappeared.

Holy ANECDOTES!

WORRYING WOUNDS

From 1919 to 1920, a physician, Dr. Luigi Romanelli, examined Padre Pio's stigmata five times. What he observed baffled him. The wounds were deep, piercing straight through the skin from one side to the other of his feet and hands. They never closed up or healed. Yet they weren't infected, nor did they have a bad smell, as another wound might. On the contrary, they emitted the scent of violets! Dr. Romanelli's diagnosis testifies to the mystification: Padre Pio's wounds did not correspond to normal surgical lesions. They were of a totally other origin, of what source, however, the doctor did not know.

FOUND GUILTY?

In 2007, the historian Sergio Luzzatto announced that he had found in the Vatican archives a note written in Padre Pio's own hand. In it, the priest asked that pure phenolic acid be used in the treatment of the poor who came to him for help. Phenolic acid can be used as an anesthetic and antiseptic (to disinfect a wound, for example), but the historian saw in this the origin of the mysterious stigmata for, after repeated applications, this acid can weaken the skin and cause it to bleed. In his eyes, Padre Pio had inflicted his wounds on himself!

✳ Mistrust Abounds ✳

The stigmata were disturbing. For some, Padre Pio seemed a fraud who had mutilated himself. To test this, Dr. Amico Bignami sealed the bandages on Padre Pio's hands. After eight days, the professor, who did not believe in God, had to acknowledge that the wounds had not changed in appearance while the priest was unable to touch them. Strange...

✳ A Sixth Wound? ✳

Padre Pio bore a sixth wound of which he spoke to no one except the Karol Wojtyla, the future Pope John Paul II. Sorting through the monk's things after his death, one of the Brothers discovered a blood stain on the right shoulder of his undershirt, at the spot where Christ would have carried his cross. This wound must have caused the Capuchin monk pain every time he removed his shirt. Observers must have thought the priest grimaced in pain because of the wound in his side, but it was surely the one in his shoulder that brought the most pain.

POPES AND THE PADRE

The popular fervor aroused by this holy man disturbed the religious authorities. They feared that the faithful might venerate this man more than Christ himself. To avoid overly large crowds of the faithful, Pope Pius XI forbade the Capuchin monk from celebrating Mass in public. Padre Pio obeyed until the pope lifted the ban. But a few years later, John XXIII, concerned by the priest's popularity, requested another in-depth investigation and reordered the ban. It was lifted once and for all by his successor, Pope Paul VI.

Déjà-vu?

Padre Pio wasn't the first in Church history to receive the stigmata. Over the course of the centuries, more than 300 persons have been identified. Not all of them were religious; laypeople have also received the stigmata. It's hard to know the exact number, even in our day, because most of these people have been extremely discreet and have not made a show of their wounds. It's an attitude that prompts one to believe the stigmata are real. On the other hand, one who trumpets his wounds and likes to display them is often a fraud.

ARE YOU SEEING DOUBLE?

Supernatural events in the life of Padre Pio are so numerous that it is difficult to list them all. For example, it's said that he had the gift of bilocation, that is, the ability to be in two places at the same time! Several witnesses have indeed reported having seen the holy man near them when he was in fact miles away behind the doors of his monastery in the company of his brother monks.

47

Above all, caution!

The stigmata manifest themselves differently in each stigmatist. Thus, the stigmata of Saint Catherine of Siena were not bloody but luminous! Rays of light emanated from her wounds. The Church has recognized the stigmata of only two saints: Saint Francis of Assisi and Saint Catherine of Siena. She remains very cautious before this phenomenon and, above all, does not force anyone to believe in it. Nor does the Church consider the stigmata proof of the holiness of a person. Holiness is demonstrated by love of God and love of others, especially the poor and the sick.

CASE no.8

A team of doctors leads the investigation!

Does Mary still work wonders at Lourdes?

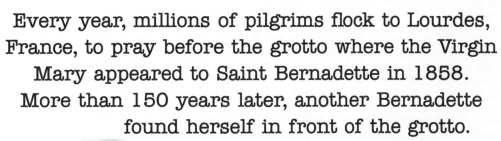

Every year, millions of pilgrims flock to Lourdes, France, to pray before the grotto where the Virgin Mary appeared to Saint Bernadette in 1858. More than 150 years later, another Bernadette found herself in front of the grotto. She was a nun on the verge of a miraculous healing...

When Sister Bernadette Moriau entered religious life—with the Franciscan Sisters Minor—she chose to train as a health worker and nurse. She had made up her mind: she would devote her life to the Lord and the sick. But, alas, things didn't go as planned. In 1966, at the age of 27, the young nun began to suffer sharp pains in her lower back.

Ever More Frail

In 1968, Sister Bernadette underwent a first operation to try to relieve her pain. The result wasn't as good as the doctors had hoped, and they operated three more times. Eventually, Sister Bernadette had to face reality: she could no longer care for the sick. In fact, she was now one of the sick herself. Little by little, the nun's condition worsened until she found herself in a wheelchair, unable to walk for very long. Her pelvis was paralyzed and her foot twisted. She wore a surgical corset and a leg splint. Her pain was so severe that she was prescribed morphine—a powerful painkiller—for almost 14 years.

In Lourdes

In July 2008, Sister Bernadette's doctor suggested that she go on pilgrimage to Lourdes with others in the diocese. Sister Bernadette wasn't expecting any miracle for herself, but she agreed to take part in the journey to ask for the healing of the sufferers traveling with her. During the pilgrimage, at adoration following the procession of the Blessed Sacrament, Sister Bernadette heard Jesus speaking to her in the depths of her heart. "I walk among you," he told her. "I see your suffering, and that of your sick brothers and sisters. Give me everything." Stunned, Sister Bernadette prayed for her sick brothers and sisters around her.

Rise and Walk

On her return home to Picardy, in northern France, Sister Bernadette went to pray in the chapel of her convent. Suddenly, she felt a great warmth and an easing throughout her body. When she returned to her room, an inner voice told her, "Remove your braces!" Moved by faith, Sister Bernadette obeyed. Her foot straightened out, her pelvis was once again supple, and her pain disappeared. She was healed. The next day, she went for a three-mile walk through the forest!

Holy ANECDOTES!

A LONG INQUIRY

The Church doesn't declare a Lourdes miracle easily. The recognition of Sister Bernadette's took 10 years! Here's the procedure:

- After a healing, the patient must go to the Lourdes Medical Office for a consultation with a doctor.
- The doctor determines whether the illness and the healing were real.
- If that's the case, the healed sufferer must compile a complete medical record. The person must then return a year later to confirm that the healing was permanent.
- Then the medical office gathers all doctors present in Lourdes (whether believers or not) for their opinions.
- If the doctors believe that there is no natural explanation for the healing, the file is passed on to the International Medical Committee of Lourdes, whose 30 doctors and specialists analyze the case and then vote by secret ballot.
- If more than two-thirds vote that the healing has no natural explanation, the news is communicated to the bishop of the diocese where the healed person resides.
- The bishop then declares — or not — that the healing is miraculous.

Only after these steps is a miracle recognized!

Symptoms

Sister Bernadette suffered from cauda equina syndrome, more colorfully known as "horsetail syndrome." It is a terrible disease of the nerve endings at the base of the spine, which are shaped like a horsetail. It's an illness with no positive prognosis. Little by little, it paralyzes the lower body. The patient can no longer walk or go to the bathroom and suffers such great pain that it requires powerful sedatives such as morphine to endure.

A Nuance of Language

The medical world never speaks of miracles; instead, it refers to an "unexplained healing in the current state of scientific knowledge." The Church alone can speak of miracles.

Subject to condition...

For a healing to be recognized as a miracle, it must meet seven criteria, known as the Lambertini criteria:

1. The illness or injury must be serious and incurable.

2. The illness must be recognized by doctors and listed among existing diseases.

3. The illness or injury must have clearly physical manifestations (unlike mental illness, for example).

4. There is no current treatment for the illness.

5. The healing is sudden and immediate.

6. The healing is total and not a simple remission of symptoms.

7. The healing is permanent. One cannot declare a healing if there is a relapse a year later.

NUMBER OF HEALINGS

The Lourdes Medical Office has identified more than 7,400 healings, either in Lourdes or immediately following a visit there. Among them, only 70 have been recognized as miraculous. In reality, it's thought there have been many more healings, because many people don't officially declare their recovery. For every physical healing that takes place at Lourdes, there are countless more healings of the heart, ones that transform a person's inner life and relationship with God.

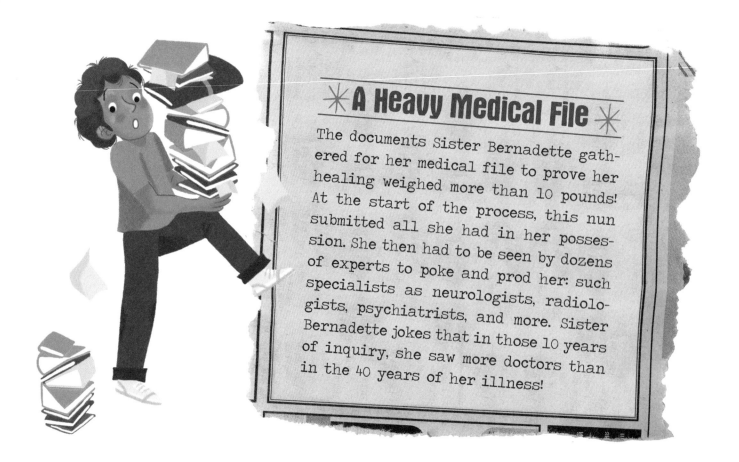

A Heavy Medical File

The documents Sister Bernadette gathered for her medical file to prove her healing weighed more than 10 pounds! At the start of the process, this nun submitted all she had in her possession. She then had to be seen by dozens of experts to poke and prod her: such specialists as neurologists, radiologists, psychiatrists, and more. Sister Bernadette jokes that in those 10 years of inquiry, she saw more doctors than in the 40 years of her illness!

✳ It's official! ✳

"Having listened to [Sister Bernadette], and taking into consideration the conclusion of the Medical Committee, and the close link between Sister Bernadette's healing and her pilgrimage to Lourdes, and, having prayed, I have determined to recognize the 'miraculous nature' of this healing as a sign from God, through the intercession of Our Lady of Lourdes. This healing reminds us of the loving and active presence of Our Lady in the life of the faithful who, like her, seek to listen to the word of God and put it into practice."

Statement of the Most Reverend
Jacques Benoît-Gonnin,
Bishop of Beauvais, Noyon, and Senlis
February 11, 2018

53

A SECOND BERNADETTE

Following the recognition of her miraculous healing, the life of Sister Bernadette went topsy-turvy: she who wished to remain behind the scenes was thrust into the limelight. From then on, everyone wanted to see her, to speak to her, to touch her. Humble and reserved, this nun still agreed to give public witness because she felt it her duty to testify to the world how much God loves his children. And it was for this reason that she agreed to submit to such a long medical inquiry. She modestly repeats the words of Saint Bernadette Soubirous following the apparitions of the Virgin Mary at the Lourdes grotto: "I was charged to tell you, not to make you believe it."

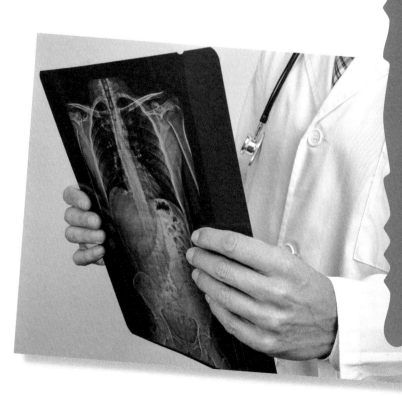

CASE no.9

Was the Host of Lanciano transformed into flesh?

It seems to have happened at Mass!

A Mass, at the moment of the Consecration, the bread and the wine truly become the Body and the Blood, the Soul and the Divinity of Christ. That's one of the fundamental beliefs of Catholic and Orthodox Christians. One day, in the 8th century, a priest began to have doubts. Then a transformation took place right before his eyes!

Basilian monks had been taking refuge for several years in the little town of Lanciano, to the east of Rome, in the Abruzzo region of Italy. In their monastery of Saint Longinus, they celebrated Mass for the local population.

True or False?

One morning, when one of the monks was celebrating Mass, he was suddenly seized by doubt. As he looked at the bread and wine, he wondered if it were really possible for two basic foodstuffs to become the Body and Blood of Jesus. After all, there was no real proof since the bread and wine don't change in appearance after the Consecration. It's a question of faith, but that was just the problem: this monk was experiencing a crisis of faith!

Living Proof

At the moment of the Consecration, while the monk was repeating the words Jesus spoke at the Last Supper, he received the proof he had been praying for. The bread was transformed into a piece of real flesh, and the wine became blood, which, when exposed to the air, rapidly coagulated into five little irregular balls or clots.

Blessed Are Those Who Believe without Seeing

The monk was speechless before this wonder. He contemplated the miracle. With both terror and amazement, he turned to the congregation, his face bathed in tears. He then showed them what had just happened and said: "O you happy faithful to whom blessed God, to confound my disbelief, has willed to reveal himself in this most holy sacrament and to make himself visible before our eyes."

The Miracle of the Mass

One can just imagine that this monk never doubted again as he celebrated Mass! And many centuries later, the faithful still come in great numbers to venerate the precious relics preserved in a crystal chalice and monstrance. Some believers see them as proof of the miracle that takes place in the Eucharist: Jesus truly offers us his Body and Blood in the consecrated bread and wine.

A Shock Team

On November 18, 1970, with the authorization of Rome, the brothers in charge of the parish where the relics are preserved decided to have them analyzed. They hoped that science could help identify what the relics are. Professor Edoardo Linoli headed the scientific inquiry. He was a professor of anatomy, histology (the study of human tissue), chemistry, and chemical microscopy—a man of some stature! And to guarantee his honesty, he was assisted by Dr. Ruggero Bertelli of the University of Siena. The two men worked on their study for almost four months.

Initial Conclusions

The results of Linoli and Bertelli's research went round the world, for they were almost unbelievable.

>> The flesh and blood are indeed of human origin. The flesh is a piece of heart tissue.

>> The blood is type AB.

But there was news even more surprising than that: over the course of their analyses, the two men compared their results with fresh blood tests. It was unthinkable, but the blood from Lanciano had exactly the same characteristics as blood drawn from a living person! And yet it was 12 centuries old! For some Catholics, the results bore a spiritual message: Jesus really is living and present in the Sacred Host. Living and risen!

A Counter-Inquiry

The results of Linoli and Bertelli's scientific analyses were so surprising that they aroused great passions in the international scientific community. In 1973, the World Health Organization, WHO, and the United Nations decided to carry out their own scientific tests to ensure there had been no deception. Following 15 months' work and 500 tests, the WHO's conclusions were the same as the two professors. In 1976, the commission announced that science was unable to provide an explanation for this phenomenon.

Holy
ANECDOTES!

What's the date?

Tradition tells us that the Eucharistic miracle of Lanciano dates back to the 8th century but doesn't specify the date or the name of the monk who witnessed the miracle. Unfortunately, as with every other century, the 8th was a hundred years long—and that's a long time! Yet, by studying history a little more closely, we find that, in 725, many priests of Greek origin arrived in Italy, settling especially near the little village of Lanciano. So we can deduce that the event probably took place between 730 and 750.

A STRANGE KIND OF JOURNEY

The relics were at first kept in the monastery of Saint Longinus. But in the 16th century, when the region was attacked by Turks, a monk worried that the relics were no longer safe there. In 1566, he moved them to the church of Lanciano, a church that had been built in 1258 and dedicated to Saint Francis. To this day, the precious relics are still preserved in Lanciano.

AN ANCIENT HOAX?

Some argue that the relics don't date back to the 8th century but were manufactured, along with the story that goes with them, during the Middle Ages.

UNBELIEVABLY WELL PRESERVED

But there's no explanation as to why they're so well preserved even after centuries of exposure to light, air, and parasites. "Normal" skin and blood would have long ago rotted and turned to dust. Scientists are firm: the flesh tissue and clots of blood were subjected to no treatment to aid their preservation or mummification.

59

A Little Vocabulary

- To believe in the **Real Presence** means to believe that Jesus is truly present in the Blessed Sacrament.
- The **sacred species** are the bread and wine consecrated at Mass to become the Body and Blood of Jesus Christ.
- **Transubstantiation**: This term is used to describe the change that takes place during the Consecration. The bread and wine are changed *substantially* to become Christ, even though they still appear to the senses as mere bread and wine. It helps to remember that since the Resurrection, Christ no longer has a body like ours. He is supernaturally present at every Mass, in every tabernacle, and in every heart that welcomes him—all at once!

A Strange Appearance

In the monstrance in Lanciano today, one can see a kind of circle of flesh with a hole in the center. In reality, the flesh appeared all around the host without totally covering it. Over the course of time, the host disappeared while the flesh remained intact. That's why there is a hole in the relic.

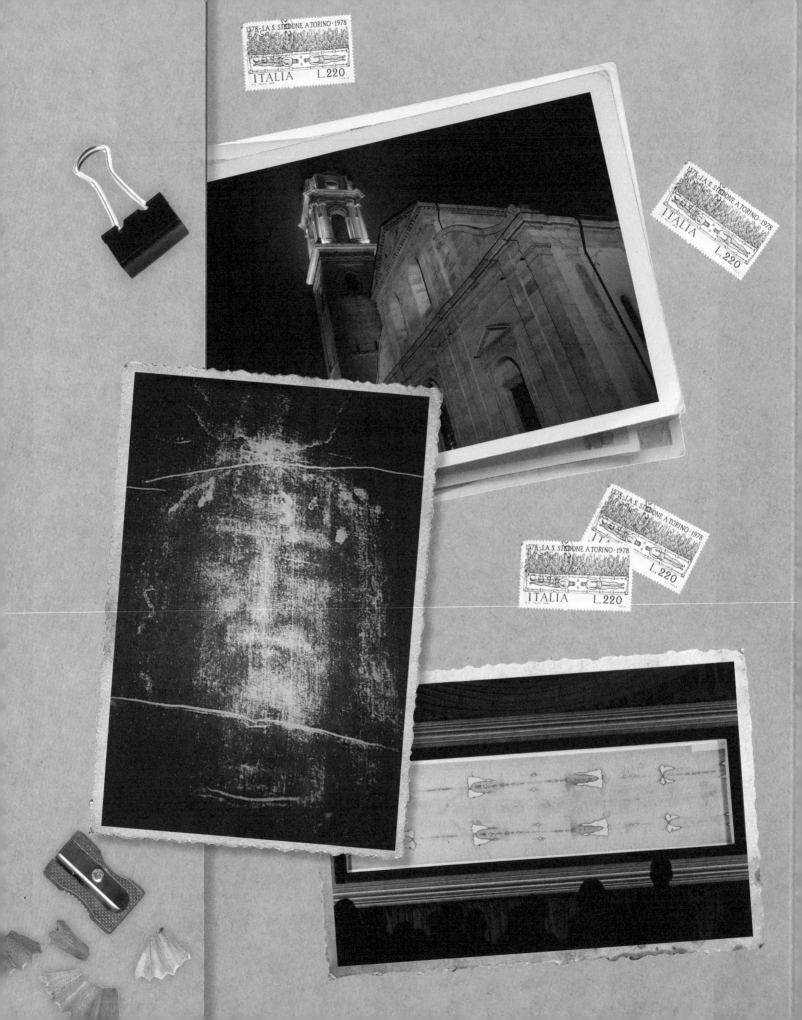

CASE no.10

What is the Shroud of Turin?

Experts line up to study it!

61

Many people—Christians and non-Christians as well—believe that the Shroud of Turin, Italy, is the burial cloth that the body of Christ was wrapped in after his death. Lost, and then found again, saved from fire, cast in doubt—its eventful history rouses many questions.

On Easter morning, when the Apostles Peter and John entered Christ's tomb, his body was not there, and the cloth he had been wrapped in was empty. Christ had risen from the dead! The Resurrection is the foundation of the Christian faith and the beginning of the story of the Shroud of Turin.

In the Beginning

Several texts from the early centuries of the Church speak of the burial cloth of Christ. They tell us it was first conserved in Jerusalem and that the Virgin Mary carefully guarded it. In 614, when the Persians invaded Palestine and pillaged the holy sites, it is supposed that this precious cloth was carried off to Constantinople along with other relics of the Passion.

The Model for Paintings

As early as the start of the 8th century, evidence of the influence of the shroud can be seen in many paintings and drawings of the crucified Jesus. Strangely, the wounds in these compositions match those on the shroud. What's more, in these paintings, there are only four fingers on both hands of Christ. just as on the shroud. These artists must certainly have seen the precious cloth!

Countless journeys

On April 13, 1204, Crusaders sacked Constantinople and took the shroud to France—first to Champagne, then Burgundy, and finally to the town of Chambéry in Savoy. There, on the night of December 3, 1532, the chapel where it was housed caught fire. Volunteers rushed into the flames to save the precious cloth, which escaped intact except for a few slightly singed spots!

A Dramatic Twist

In 1578, the shroud arrived in Turin on the occasion of a pilgrimage. And there it was to remain. But everything took a new turn when Secondo Pia photographed it. On the negative, the face of a tortured man appeared even clearer than it did on the cloth itself! The cloth immediately became the object of study for many scientists determined to prove it authentic or phony!

Holy ANECDOTES!

A TROUBLING DATING

In 1988, three laboratories were commissioned to analyze and date the Shroud of Turin. At the time, the carbon-14 dating technique was used, and the results of the three laboratories were in agreement: the shroud dated from the Middle Ages. It was probably woven between 1260 and 1390. Thus, to the scientists, the shroud was a fake.

So what is carbon-14?

There are many forms of carbon in nature, including carbon-14, which is radioactive. There's carbon-14 in any object made of organic matter (for example, in plants from which we extract fibers). As long as the matter remains alive, the carbon-14 remains the same. But when it dies, the amount of carbon-14 decreases with precise regularity over time. By calculating the quantity of carbon-14 in a fiber, one can then determine its age.

The Fabric Speaks

In 2005, the Swiss textile historian Mechthild Flury-Lemberg asserted that the dating in 1988 was unreliable. She was concerned about the dust on the edges of the shroud, which could have been deposited when the cloth was put on public display. She also noted that a seam on the shroud was characteristic of that used in 1st century Palestine. In her opinion, although these observations were not enough to confirm its authenticity, they certainly meant the shroud didn't date from the Middle Ages.

A New Turnaround

On May 23, 2019, the age of the shroud was again called into question. An Italian statistician and a group of experts also cast doubt on the results of the 1988 researchers. In their view, the results were distorted by the use of products used to clean the shroud during its long history.

FIRST ANALYSES

In 1978, a group of American scientists decided to analyze the relic. There were many skeptics among them who expected to find that it was a fake. But, after weeks of research, this was their observation: "We can conclude for now that the Shroud image is that of a real human form of a scourged, crucified man. It is not the product of an artist. The blood stains are composed of hemoglobin and also give a positive test for serum albumin." The blood is that of an AB group male, the same blood group as that of the Eucharistic blood of Lanciano (see page 55). It was estimated that the man was between 30 and 35 years of age—according to tradition, Christ had died at 33—and that he was between 5.8 and 5.9 feet tall and weighed about 176 pounds.

A BIT OF NATURE

Scientists have been working to identify the traces of pollen in the shroud. Some of these researchers are fierce opponents of its authenticity, and yet, out of the 58 species found, they agree that 44 originate in the Mediterranean basin, and that 28 bloom in the spring, between Jerusalem and Jericho.

A Hasty Burial

The body wrapped in the shroud had not been washed, contrary to Jewish custom in the days of Christ. So burial must have been done in a hurry, as Christ's was because he died on the eve of the Sabbath. We also know that those condemned to death for crimes against religion or who had suffered a violent, bloody death sometimes were buried unwashed.

✳ Dusty Samples ✳

Dust particles have been found on the shroud. They're located in the area of the nose, the knees, and the feet. The dust is from aragonite, a stone used in Jerusalem.

A Little Vocabulary

This precious cloth has its own vocabulary. The study of the Shroud of Turin is called "sindology." A sindon is a textile that serves as a veil, a cloth, a dress, or, as here, a shroud. Sindology brings together 25 different disciplines. It is practiced by both atheistic scientists as well as those of many religions.

THAT'S NOT SERIOUS!

In July 2018, two researchers asserted that half the blood droplets on the shroud couldn't be authentic. According to them, they don't flow in a logical pattern. The Vatican immediately reacted to this new study, which hadn't been carried out according to scientific methods. For, though the two researchers had indeed carried out their tests using human blood, they had done so on a plastic dummy.

THE TRACES OF TORTURE

The traces of wounds found on the shroud leave little room for doubt about the manner in which this man was put to death. They correspond to those described in the accounts of the Passion.

- There are 120 lashes of the flagellum, a whip with several strands whose ends are weighted with lead or bits of bone.
- The nose is swollen.
- The shoulders are bloodied from the carrying of a cross.
- The face is swollen, with a rip in the right eyelid.
- The head bears the marks of a crown of thorns.
- There are nail wounds in the wrists and the feet. (Three nails were used for the crucifixion, one in each wrist and one in the superimposed feet.)
- There is one wound in the side, of the dimensions of a Roman pilum (or lance).

A RELIGIOUS PAINTING

In 1389, the bishop of Troyes, France, was convinced that the shroud was a fake. He is said to have written to Pope Clement VII to state that it was merely a cloth skillfully painted with the double image of a man, intended to trick people into paying money to see it.
Since then, dozens of copies of the shroud have been produced. Yet, none has succeeded in exactly reproducing what is found in the Shroud of Turin, even with methods and techniques far more developed than those of the Middle Ages.

That's a bit fishy!

It's strange that the man on the Shroud of Turin seems to have only four fingers on each hand. But historians and doctors easily explain this: the nails of the crucifixion were driven into the wrists, where they hold best. When the nerves are hit, the thumbs retract toward the palm, leaving only four fingers visible!

CASE no.11

How does the blood of Saint Januarius liquefy?

Apparently, the miracle occurs every year!

Saint Januarius is the patron saint of the city of Naples, Italy, where his precious relics are preserved. In addition to his bones, two vials of his blood excite fervor because, with any luck, several times a year, the dried blood turns liquid again...

On Saint Januarius feast day, September 19, the people of the city of Naples gather inside the cathedral and outside on the plaza. They come to witness the miracle of Saint Januarius, the patron of the city. All eyes are fixed on the round reliquary carried by the bishop. It is believed to contain two vials of the saint's blood.

A Blessed Year

Saint Januarius was martyred in the year 305, so it's been a long time since his blood had solidified in these vials. And yet, three times a year, the blood inexplicably turns back into liquid. That's the miracle the people of Naples wait eagerly to see.

The Wait for the Miracle

The bishop of Naples lowers the reliquary to the left and then to the right. The blood remains immobile, stuck to the sides of the vials. In the cathedral, there is deep silence. The faithful redouble their prayers. The bishop moves the reliquary again. Still nothing... "Saint Januarius, rejoice us!" the faithful clamor. And then, suddenly, the blood seems to move a little. A little smile forms on the bishop's lips. At the back of the cathedral, no one can see anything. But when the treasury official standing behind the bishop at last waves a white handkerchief, the whole congregation erupts in relieved applause. The miracle has taken place!

A Miracle in the Distance

In the cathedral, the police commissioner scrupulously notes down the time it took for the miracle to take place. The liquefaction of the blood can take a few hours, and sometimes days. The bishop then slowly processes up and down the aisles of the cathedral. Outside, the bells ring out at full blast to announce the news to the whole city.

THE LIFE OF SAINT JANUARIUS

The bishop Saint Januarius lived in the 4th century, when persecutions of Christians were ordered by the Roman emperor Diocletian. Because the saintly bishop encouraged Christians to stand firm against the oppressor and to accept martyrdom if necessary, he himself was martyred. He was thrown into a furnace but escaped unharmed. Then he was thrown to the lions, and the animals refused to attack him. Impatient with the bishop's refusal to die, the Roman officials ordered that he be beheaded. When the saint—at long last!—died, one of his female relatives gathered up a little of his blood on a sponge and placed it in two vials. It is this blood that today attracts the crowds.

 ## A Forecast in a Vial

Neapolitans impatiently await the miracle of Saint Januarius, for many see in it signs for the year to come. To them, if the blood quickly liquefies, it's an excellent sign for the coming year. If, on the other hand, it remains solidified or takes a long time to liquefy, you can expect misfortunes.

69

TECHNICALLY SPEAKING

When blood solidifies and dries, it is possible to liquefy it again. It just takes adding some alcohol. The result is immediate, but the blood can then no longer solidify again. So the experiment can only be done once and for all—not three times a year for centuries!

Three Times a Year

The miracle of the liquefaction of the blood of Saint Januarius occurs on the first Sunday of May, in commemoration of the day the saint's relics entered Naples, and on September 19, the anniversary of the saint's death. More rarely, it also occurs on December 16, the date of the eruption of Mount Vesuvius in 1631, when the city of Naples was spared. It has also occurred on the occasion of the visit of an important person to the city.

A Good Sense of Humor

In 2015, Pope Francis visited Naples. When the relics were brought out to renew the miracle of the blood before him, the blood in the vials only half liquefied. The pope remarked, "The saint only half loves us," so we must convert twice as hard. It must be said, the pope has a good sense of humor.

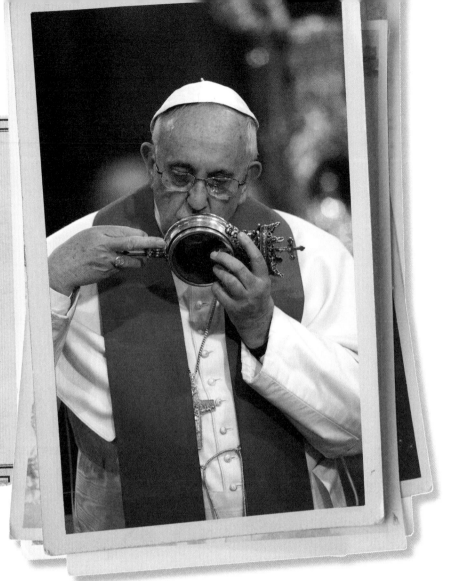

Great Misfortunes

In 1526 and 1527, the blood didn't liquefy, and the city of Naples was the victim of a raging epidemic of the plague. In December 1943, once again the miracle failed to happen, and four months later, the nearby Mount Vesuvius began to erupt. The same failure occurred in September 1980, and it was followed by an earthquake.

FICKLE NATURE

The liquefied blood doesn't seem to respect any of the laws of nature. It liquefies whether it's hot or cold; it sometimes even boils! Sometimes, the blood increases in volume; sometimes it reduces. The reliquary is weighed before the miracle. When it is weighed again after the miracle, it's either heavier or lighter. The color of the blood changes as well: it's dark brown to start with and then becomes more and more bright red as the miracle occurs.

THE BEGINNING OF A PROOF?

Over the course of the centuries, researchers of all disciplines have tried to determine what's inside the vials. They've considered substances that freely liquefy and solidify simply by shaking them. Some have even looked at powdered chocolate! Others, more seriously, have considered only materials known in the Middle Ages. But the evidence is insufficient. If it's a purely chemical or mechanical process, then what explains that sometimes the miracle doesn't occur?

✳ Not without Risk ✳

For skeptics, it would be enough to settle doubts if one could test a sample of the liquid in the vials of Saint Januarius. Then they could see if it is, in fact, human blood. But they recognize that such an experiment would not be without great risk. The blood has been enclosed in vials for such a long time that opening them could cause an unknown reaction. And if the blood of Saint Januarius were to disappear, the city of Naples would be up in arms!

71

Very, very strange...

In Naples and its surrounding area, Saint Januarius isn't the only one to work wonders through his blood. There are several other saints whose blood liquefies in the same way. That's fuel for the fire of skeptics, because all of these saints lived after 1389, the date of the first written testimony of the miracle of Saint Januarius. So are they perhaps copycats?

CASE no.12

Where are the bones of Saint Peter buried?

They're not in this amphora!

Does the body of Peter, the Apostle of Jesus and the first pope of the Church, lie within the magnificent basilica in Rome that bears his name?
The search for the tomb of Saint Peter is a real enigma that has gone on for centuries!

The City of Rome Is in Flames!

Rome had been burning for nine days before the eyes of Emperor Nero, who dreamed of rebuilding it to be even more beautiful and grand. But the population didn't see this devastating fire in the same way: they were terrified and wanted someone to blame for the catastrophe. Gossip spread that it was Nero himself who had set fire to the city. In order to defend himself, he pointed the finger at the perfect scapegoats: the Christians.

The Manhunt Begins

Thus began a roundup of Christians. At first, just a few were taken and locked up, but then more and more followed. Some were denounced by jealous neighbors, others by treacherous friends terrified at the idea of being carted off themselves. Among them was Peter, the Apostle of Jesus, upon whom Christ had chosen to build his Church.

On the Games Program

These arrests came at a good time for Nero: to celebrate the 10th anniversary of his accession to the throne, he had organized sumptuous circus games. He was now planning a great spectacle for the people of Rome: Christians would be sacrificed in the arena of the Circus of Nero, not far from the present-day Saint Peter's Square. The Apostle Peter was to be one of the highlights of the spectacle. A special death was reserved for him: a crucifixion.

Martyrdom

And so it was that Saint Peter died, in A.D. 64, crucified like Jesus, whom he so loved to the end. But the Apostle insisted that he was unworthy of dying in the same way as his Lord. He asked to be crucified upside down.

A First Burial Place

Peter was buried directly in the ground just outside the circus. Some years later, a temple-shaped shrine called a "trophy" was built over the spot. A 2nd-century letter by a priest named Gaius states that Peter was buried in this location.

A Hasty Removal?

In 258, Emperor Valerian ordered a new round of persecutions. Fearing that the tomb of Saint Peter would be desecrated, Christians might have transferred Peter's remains to the Catacomb of Saint Sebastian, along with those of the Apostle Paul. There they might have stayed hidden until after Emperor Constantine legalized Christianity in 313.

A Christian Emperor

In 320, Emperor Constantine decided to honor Saint Peter by building a basilica over his tomb. Ideally, it would have been constructed a little farther away from where the Apostle was originally buried, for his tomb had been located on sloping ground. Building there would mean demolishing the Vatican Circus and razing the Roman cemetery. That would be no easy task. But the emperor insisted that the basilica be in that location, and that was where it was built.

The Present Basilica

After many centuries, Constantine's basilica was on the verge of falling into ruins. At the start of the 16th century, Pope Julius II decided to replace it with a new, much larger building. It took more than 100 years to complete, and the greatest artists of the time made it magnificent. Yet over all that time, the location of Saint Peter's tomb became uncertain.

Packages of Bones

In the 20th century, several excavations took place beneath Saint Peter's Basilica. From around 1940 to 1942, archeologists removed bones, which had been placed in crates... and forgotten about.

Strange Graffiti

On December 24, 1950, Pope Pius XII announced that the resting place of Saint Peter had been found. Within the current Saint Peter's Basilica, archeologists had, they believed, identified the tomb of Saint Peter by some graffiti stating, "Saint Peter lies within." Except that... the tomb was empty!

It Is Written...

In 1952, a university professor specializing in Greek graffiti, Margherita Guarducci, wished to study the famous text on the wall of the tomb. She requested authorization from the Vatican to enter the crypt to carry out her research. But, alas, the graffiti had disappeared! It seems that the one who had discovered it wished to keep the discovery to himself. But the professor didn't give up. She deciphered another inscription that confirmed that the tomb of the Apostle was indeed there: "Peter, pray to Christ Jesus for the holy Christian men buried near your body." But there was still no body.

A New Discovery

It was while questioning those who knew the site best that Margherita Guarducci discovered the existence of bones that had previously been removed from the tomb and stored in crates. In one of the crates, the bones were very fragile, whitened, and encrusted with soil. Among some of them, the professor noticed a few remains of red fabric with gold threads. Could this be the start of a possible lead?

Victory!

It would take another 10 years for the bones in the crate to at last be analyzed. When the results were published, the bones were those of a man of about 60 or 70 of a robust constitution; a man who had long worked on the water (like a fisherman), who was missing the bones in his hands and feet (like other crucified Christians whose hands and feet were cut off to remove them quickly from the wood of the cross). It was just one step between this discovery and realizing that these were the bones of Saint Peter.

Holy
ANECDOTES!

 ## A Good Reason

Romans have great respect for the dead and would not have razed a cemetery unless it was for a really good reason. As the cemetery was razed by the emperor's orders, it seems that the site being Saint Peter's tomb would be that good reason.

IN THE SAME SOIL

Some of the bones found in the crate were encrusted with soil. An analysis of the soil's composition showed that it matched the soil around the basilica, where the saint had been buried in a hurry, immediately after his death. Just one more clue!

THE RED COLOR

Some of the bones found in the crate have red coloration in places. It was discovered that the bones had been wrapped in a red fabric with golden threads. Golden thread wasn't common: it was a rare commodity! That's a clear sign that these bones belonged to someone important.

At the Foot of the Obelisk

The place of the death of Saint Peter has today been established, for several authors refer to it in their texts. Nero's Circus, also referred to as the Circus Vaticanus, was situated a few yards from the present Basilica of Saint Peter. In the center of this vast edifice stood an obelisk, a pillar, surrounded by two markers, and it was exactly between those two markers that Saint Peter was crucified. That very obelisk is in the center of Saint Peter's Square today.

An Official Announcement

On June 26, 1968, Pope Paul VI proclaimed that the true relics of Saint Peter had been identified below the Basilica of Saint Peter. It is just as Jesus had announced to Peter, "You are Peter, and upon this rock I will build my church" (Matthew 16:18).

Your turn to investigate!

Do you know where these details can be found?

1

2

3

4

5

6

ANSWERS: **1.** Detail of the habit of Padre Pio (p. 42). **2.** Saint Peter's Basilica (p. 43). **3.** Crystal chalice containing part of the relics of Lanciano (p. 54). **4.** The crowd awaiting the miracle of Saint Januarius before the Cathedral of Naples (p. 66). **5.** The crown of the Virgin of Fatima (p. 30). **6.** The feet of Saint Francis-Xavier (p. 21). **7.** The split column of the Holy Sepulchre (p. 24). **8.** The village of Rocamadour (p. 6). **9.** Detail of Our Lady of Guadalupe (p. 15). **10.** Detail of the grotto of Lourdes (p. 48). **11.** Detail of the Shroud of Turin (p. 63). **12.** Chapel of Loretto in New Mexico (p. 36).

Photographic Credits

Printed in July 2021 by DZS, in Ljubljana, Slovenia
Job number MGN 21038-02
Printed in compliance with the Consumer
Protection Safety Act, 2008